THE CURIOSITY BOX

ANIMALS

by Peter Riley

Illustrated by Krina Patel

W

FRANKLIN WATTS

LONDON • SYDNEY

Franklin Watts
Published in paperback in Great Britain in 2019 by The Watts Publishing Group

Credits
Series Editor: Amy Stephenson
Series Designer: Krina Patel
Illustrations: Krina Patel
Picture Researcher: Amy Stephenson / Diana Morris

Picture Credits: AAlex81/Shutterstock: 15t. Stacey Ann Alberts/Shutterstock: 17c. Hintau Aliaksei/Shutterstock: 5tlc. Andrew Astburg/Dreamstime: 16ca. Nick Biemans/Dreamstime: 24t. Blickwinkel/Alamy: 7b, 28bla. John Caremolia/Shutterstock: 22b. Coprid/Shutterstock: back cover cr, 5br. Djavitch/Shutterstock: 9t. Double Brow Imagery/Shutterstock: 21t. Michal Durinik/Shutterstock: 10b. Emi/Shutterstock: 4b. Eyeblink/Shutterstock: 5tcl. file404/Shutterstock: 27tl. Susan Flashman/Shutterstock: 16c. Ekaterina Fribus/Dreamstime: 15b, 29bla. Sanit Fuangnakhou/Shutterstock: 27b. Joseph Fuller/Dreamstime: 24b. Gavran333/Shutterstock: back cover t, 5cl. Hariz/Dreamstime: 23t. Hergon/Shutterstock: 21b. Hkratky/Dreamstime: 9cl. Jiang Hongyan/Shutterstock: 5tr. Vitalii Hulai/Shutterstock: 13tr. Isselee/Dreamstime: 5tcr. Eric Isselee/Shutterstock: front cover bl, 17tb, 25b, 29bl. JA?AjnosNA?©meth/Shutterstock: 26t. Jannarong/Shutterstock: 15c. Rosa Jay/Shutterstock: 27tr. Jessamine/Shutterstock: 5cr. Evgeny Karaadaev/Shutterstock: front cover br, 5bc. Aleksey Karpouko/Shutterstock: 19t, 19cl. Kletr/Shutterstock: 9b. Heidi & Hans Juergen Koch/Minden Pictures/FLPA: 16t. Zdenek Kubik/Shutterstock: 6br. Laborant/Shutterstock: 17b. Mike Lane45/Dreamstime: 25t. Brian Lasenby/Shutterstock: 21c. Lestertaiv/Shutterstock: front cover bcl, 8bc. Yury Mansiliya/Shutterstock: 5tl. Mokvijpers/Dreamstime: 13b. Nature PL/Alamy: 8br. Ninell/Shutterstock: 9cr. Maciej Oiszewski/Shutterstock: back cover cl, 5bl, 28bc. Songsak Paname/Dreamstime: 19b, 29bra. Pratik Panda/Dreamstime: 14t. Picstudio/Dreamstime: 18tl. Alexander Popatov/Shutterstock: 18tr. Alexander Potapov/Dreamstime: 18br. Dave Pressland/FLPA: 6bl. Stephen Rees/Shutterstock: 23b, 28bl. reptiles4all/Shutterstock: 16b. Mauro Rodrigues/Shutterstock: 25c. Roman Samokhin/Shutterstock: 17t. Sauletas/Shutterstock: 11t. Shelley Still/Shutterstock: front cover b, 25ca, 29br. Marek R Swadzba/Shutterstock: 13c. Taivi/Shutterstock: 26b. Paul Tessier/Shutterstock: 14c. THPStock/Shutterstock: 18cl. Tomas1111/Dreamstime: 19cr. Victor Tyakht/Shutterstock: 21cr. Sergey Uryadnikov/Dreamstime: 7tl. Tomas Valenta, Bm Association/Dreamstime: 10t. Steven van Verre/Shutterstock: 21cl. Delmot Vivian/Shutterstock: 26c. VladaPhoto/Shutterstock: 7tr. Woe/Shutterstock: 11b, 28bca. Rudmer Zwerver/Dreamstime: 13tl.

ISBN: 978 1 4451 4639 3
Printed in China

To Jackie and Roger – PR
To June and Maurice Sage – KP

Franklin Watts
An imprint of
Hachette Children's Group
Part of The Watts Publishing Group
Carmelite House
50 Victoria Embankment
London EC4Y 0DZ

An Hachette UK Company
www.hachette.co.uk
www.franklinwatts.co.uk

CONTENTS

⚠ This symbol shows where there is some information to help you stay safe around animals. Words in **bold** can be found in the glossary on page 30.

WHAT ARE ANIMALS?

Animals are living things. They live in places called habitats. A seashore, pond, field and wood are some types of animal habitats. All animals move about and feed.

You can find out many curious things about animals in this book. Sometimes you have to guess what you see, then turn the page to find the answer.

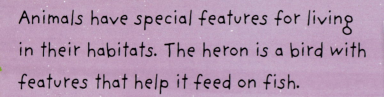

Animals have special features for living in their habitats. The heron is a bird with features that help it feed on fish.

Near the end of this book is our animals curiosity box. You can talk about it with your friends. You can make your own curiosity box about animals if you visit a garden or a park or the countryside.

A heron has long legs for wading in water and a pointed beak to catch fish.

Vertebrate (ver-tih-brate) animals have a **skeleton** inside their bodies. This book is about them. Vertebrates are divided into five groups: fish, amphibians (am-fib-ee-ans), reptiles, birds and mammals.

fish

frog – amphibian

snake – reptile

bird

rabbit – mammal

Sometimes you may find things that belonged to an animal or things that an animal made.

Which of these items are *parts* of an animal? Which items were *made by* an animal?

skull

nest

frogspawn

egg

feather

FISH

Fish live in watery habitats. They have **fins** and **gills**. Most fish have **scales**, too. Fish don't **breathe** in air, they breathe in water through their gills.

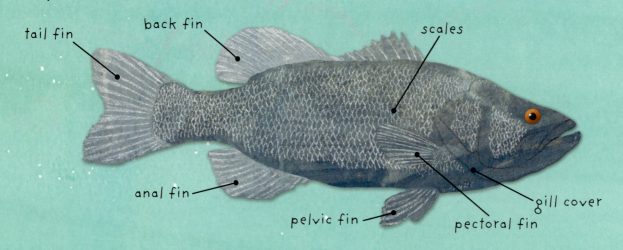

tail fin

back fin

scales

anal fin

pelvic fin

pectoral fin

gill cover

There are two kinds of watery habitat on Earth — FRESHWATER and SALTWATER. Rain forms freshwater ponds, streams and rivers. The rivers flow into seas and oceans where there is salt. This makes seas and oceans saltwater habitats.

Most fish live in either a freshwater or a saltwater habitat. These fish live in freshwater.

The bullhead is a fish that lives in fast-flowing rivers. It hides under stones to stop being washed away.

The carp is a fish that lives in slow-flowing rivers and ponds.

These fish live in saltwater.

The great white shark is a very large fish. It feeds near the surface of the sea.

Cod live near the seabed. They feed on crabs, lobsters and other fish, such as haddock.

WHAT CAN THIS BE?

A snake?
A young fish?
A water worm?
Turn the page to find out.

It's a young fish!

The fish is a young EEL called a glass eel. Its body is see-through. When it grows into an adult eel, you can no longer see through it.

An eel is a fish with a long, bendy body. It swims by moving its body a bit like a snake does.

Adult eels leave rivers and swim out to sea where they lay their eggs. Eels can live in both freshwater and saltwater.

Fish called SALMON start life as eggs in a freshwater river.

When they hatch, the young salmon live in rivers for up to three years.

salmon eggs

a par (a young salmon)

In the US, brown bears catch some of the salmon as they swim upstream to breed.

Then the young salmon live in the sea for up to five years. When they are ready to **BREED**, they swim back up the same river where they were born.

You can tell the age of a fish by looking at its SCALES. Fish scales grow a ring every year.

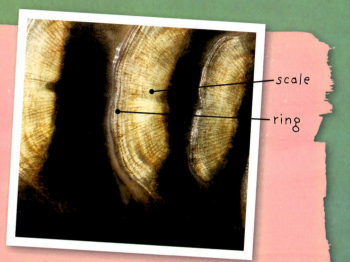

scale

ring

The patterns on this trout's scales help it hide among the plants in this river.

Some fish have PATTERNS of colour on their scales. The patterns help them hide away from **predators**.

The PIKE only lives in freshwater. It has a mouth full of sharp teeth and eats all the fish it can find, including eel, salmon and trout!

The pike is a big, agressive fish. It will even attack and eat water birds!

AMPHIBIANS

Amphibians are animals that mainly live in water as young and on land as adults.

Young amphibians are born in water. They look a little like fish, but they do not have scales. Adult amphibians live on land, but return to water to lay their eggs and breed.

Frogs are amphibians with wet skin that feels slimy.

FROGS have long back legs and can make high jumps.

Some adult **rainforest** frogs don't live on land or in water. They live in trees. They have bright colours. The colours warn predators that they are **poisonous**.

TOADS are amphibians with rough, dry skin. Toads have short back legs that help the toads run and hop.

The bumps on a toads skin are sometimes called '**warts**', but they are not real warts.

WHAT CAN THIS BE?

A currant

A young frog's head

A stone

Turn the page to find out.

TADPOLES
It's a young frog's head!

All amphibians have a tadpole stage in their **life cycle**.
This is the stage when they live in water.
Here is the life cycle of a frog.

1. The tadpole hatches out of its egg (frogspawn).

2. At first, the tadpole has gills outside its head.

6. The froglet grows into an adult frog. Female frogs lay frogspawn.

5. The tadpole **absorbs** its tail and changes into a froglet.

3. In time, the gills grow inside the body and the tadpole grows legs.

4. Inside the tadpole, **lungs** form and take the place of the gills. This means the frog can now breathe air and live on land.

LONG-BODY AMPHIBIANS

NEWTS are amphibians with long bodies. They visit ponds in the springtime to breed. Many newts live on land for the rest of the year. The male newt has a crest along its back and tail.

crest

male

female

FIRE SALAMANDERS are related to newts. They hide away in logs in forests in central Europe. Long ago, people believed that fire salamanders lived in fire. When logs were burned, the fire salamanders would crawl out!

Fire salamanders have beautiful black-and-yellow patterned skin.

A caecilian cannot see well. Its eyes are covered with skin that protects them as it burrows.

CAECILIANS (see-sil-ee-uns) live mainly in **burrows** in rainforests. They do not have any legs and are the only amphibians to have **tentacles** on their head.

REPTILES

Reptiles have bodies covered in dry scales. Most reptiles are **cold-blooded** and they have to warm their blood before they can move about. They do this by **basking** in the sun.

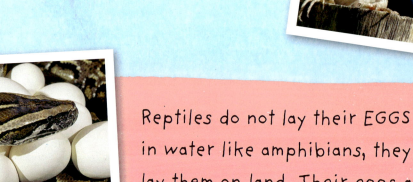

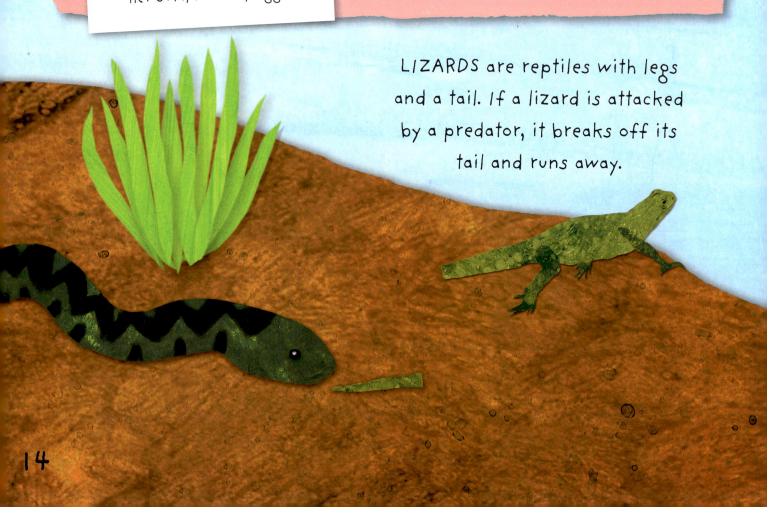

This mother snake is guarding her soft, leathery eggs.

Reptiles do not lay their EGGS in water like amphibians, they lay them on land. Their eggs are covered in a shell, which may be either leathery or hard.

LIZARDS are reptiles with legs and a tail. If a lizard is attacked by a predator, it breaks off its tail and runs away.

Later it grows a new tail.

Geckos have special pads on their toes that help them 'stick' to walls and ceilings.

GECKOS are lizards that live in warm places around the world. They have pads on their feet that let them easily climb up walls and trees, and walk across ceilings.

WHAT CAN THIS BE?

A leaf?
A dead snake?
A snake skin?
Turn the page to find out.

It's a snake skin!

Snakes are reptiles without any legs. As they grow, they shed all of their old SKIN in one piece. New skin is underneath the old skin.

A snake sticks out its FORKED TONGUE to taste the air. It does this to find **prey** animals, such as mice and birds.

Snakes don't chew their food, they SWALLOW it whole!

All snakes have teeth but **venomous** snakes have FANGS.

The fangs swing forward as the snake bites. They inject poison into the prey animal to kill it.

⚠ If you see a snake, stay away from it and do not touch it.

CROCODILES and ALLIGATORS are big reptiles with large, pointed teeth.

crocodile

alligator

scutes

You can tell them apart by looking at their HEADS. A crocodile has a long, pointed head. An alligator has a shorter, rounded head

Crocodiles and alligators have skin covered in bumpy, bony scales — called SCUTES. They form a suit of armour to protect the animal.

Tortoises and turtles have large, flat scutes. The scutes lock together, like pieces of a jigsaw puzzle, to make a dome-shaped SHELL.

A tortoise lives on land. When it sleeps it draws its head, legs and tail into its shell.

Turtles live most of their lives in water. They have flat shells and webbed feet. They cannot draw themselves into their shells.

BIRDS

Birds are animals with two wings, two legs, a beak, and a body covered with feathers.

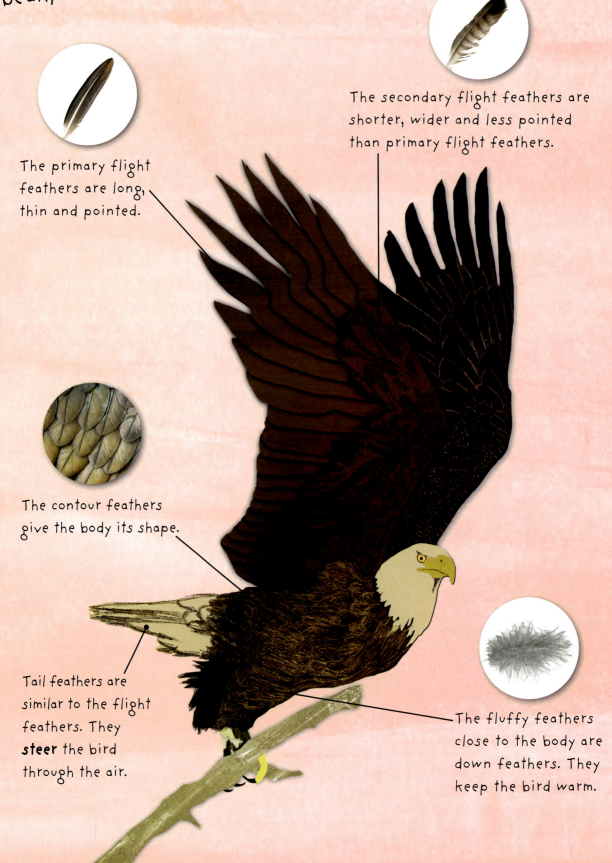

The primary flight feathers are long, thin and pointed.

The secondary flight feathers are shorter, wider and less pointed than primary flight feathers.

The contour feathers give the body its shape.

Tail feathers are similar to the flight feathers. They **steer** the bird through the air.

The fluffy feathers close to the body are down feathers. They keep the bird warm.

Birds' feathers can be many COLOURS. Some make patterns, which can be used to **identify** the bird. The starling has black feathers that look green and purple when light shines on them.

MALE birds are usually more colourful than FEMALES. Male birds use their colourful feathers to attract females.

male mallard duck

female mallard duck

WHAT CAN THIS BE?

A bird's nest?
An upside down basket?
A strange flower?
Turn the page to find out.

NESTS, AND BIRDS IN ACTION
It's a bird's nest!
The nest builder is a weaver bird that lives in India.

Nearly all birds build nests. Some weave together MATERIALS, such as twigs and grass, which they find nearby.

A NEST is a safe place for birds' eggs and chicks. Both parent birds may take turns sitting on the eggs to keep them warm.

The chick inside each egg needs warmth to help it grow. When a chick is ready to hatch, it taps on the inside of the shell with its beak.

Many birds' eggs are white or a single colour, such as blue. They may also have a few speckles.

Birds that nest on the ground have patterns spots and lines on them. These make the eggs hard for predators to see if the parent birds are away from the nest.

Most birds are active during the day. Like us, they cannot see well in the dark.

Every day of the year you can see birds walking on the ground, hopping in the trees and flying around their habitats searching for food.

In spring, male birds like this thrush sing loudly to attract a **mate**.

Birds' beaks are shaped to help them feed.

A finch has a blunt beak to crush seeds.

A wren has a pointed beak to pull insects out of cracks in tree **bark**.

A bird of prey, such as an osprey, has a hooked beak to tear up meat.

A few birds, such as OWLS, have very big eyes and can see well in the dark. They fly and hunt for food at night.

Owls have special feathers on their wings that stop the wing making a sound as the owl flies. Prey animals cannot hear the owl coming.

The owl listens for prey moving on the ground, then swoops down to catch it.

MAMMALS

Mammals can be very small like the mouse or very big like the elephant. Mammals are **warm-blooded**. They have skin that grows hair and most baby mammals grow inside their mothers until they are ready to be born. Afterwards their mothers give them milk to help them grow.

The largest mammal is the BLUE WHALE. It lives in the ocean. Mammals are found in almost every habitat, from goats grazing on mountain tops to bears sleeping in forests. There is even a mammal reading this book — you!

goat

blue whale

The PLATYPUS is a very strange mammal. It has a mouth like a duck's beak and it lays eggs! Platypus babies hatch from the eggs.

Some mammal mothers have a **POUCH.**
Tiny newborn babies climb into the pouch
and grow there instead of inside the
mother. Later, the babies leave the pouch
but stay with the mother for some time.

The kangaroo is a mammal that
has a baby in a pouch. A baby
kangaroo is called a joey.

bear

WHAT CAN THIS BE?

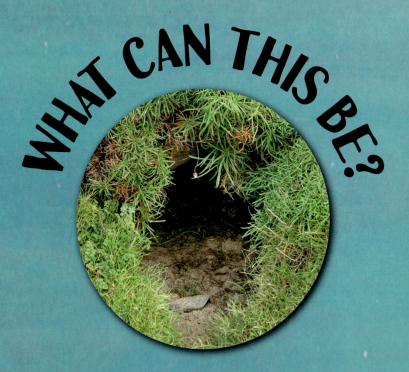

A small cave?
A hole made by a plant?
A burrow?
Turn the page to find out.

BURROWS, NESTS AND SKULLS!

It's a burrow!

Many mammals dig BURROWS and make a nest in them for their babies to live in.

baby rabbits outside their burrow

MOLES live in burrows all their lives. They leave piles of soil, called molehills, where they have been burrowing.

mole

molehill

Other mammals build nests from materials. The squirrel makes a nest called a DREY in a tree. It is made from twigs and leaves.

Why does it make a drey? Is it for its young or is it to stay warm in the winter — or both?

The harvest mouse makes a nest in tall grass. The nest is made of grass, too!

Sometimes, people walking in the countryside find mammal skulls.

The rabbit skull has two pairs of teeth at the front of the jaw.

The sheep skull has no teeth in the front of its upper jaw.

WHAT CAN THIS BE?

An antler?
A branch?
A strange leg?
Turn the page to find out.

ANTLERS AND HORNS

It's an antler!

ANTLERS are made of bone. They usually only grow on a male deer's head. Males use them to attract female deer for breeding and to fight other males. Whenever the antlers fall off, a deer grows new, bigger ones.

Male red deer fight with their antlers to see which of them is the biggest and strongest.

Cows have HORNS. The horns have bone inside them, but are covered in a hard, shiny material called keratin (keh-rah-tin). Keratin also makes our nails and hair.

horn

The horn of a rhino does not have any bone inside. It is only made of keratin.

FINGERS AND WINGS

Many mammals have hooves (horses) or paws (cats),
but monkeys, apes and humans have hands and fingers.

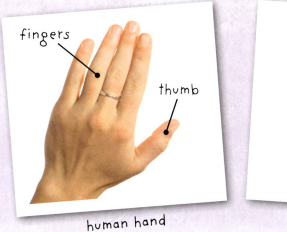

fingers

thumb

human hand

thumb

fingers

monkey hand

Bats also have hands and fingers. Their wings are
made from skin stretched between their fingers!

Bats rest all day and fly around
trees and buildings in the evening to
find moths and other insects to eat.

ANIMALS CURIOSITY BOX

A curiosity box is a place to put all of the curious things you have collected.

What items are in your animals curiosity box?

glass eel

tadpole

burrow

frogspawn

antler

CURIOUS QUIZ

1. Which fish lives in saltwater?
a) a carp
b) a pike
c) a shark

2. Which animal group does a saalamander belong to?
a) mammals
b) amphibians
c) reptiles

3. Which animal can climb up walls?
a) a gecko
b) a rhino
c) a blue whale

4. What happens if a deer's antler falls off?
a) it grows another, bigger one
b) it grows another, smaller one
c) the other antler grows twice as big

5. What does a down feather do?
a) it helps a bird to fly
b) it helps a bird to sing
c) it keeps a bird's body warm

6. Which animals makes a burrow?
a) a goat
b) a mole
c) a bat

Curious quiz answers: 1c; 2b; 3a; 4a; 5c; 6b.

On page 5, the items made by an animal are: nest, egg and frogspawn. The items that are part of an animal are: skull and feather. A squirrel's drey (page 24) is used for both keeping young safe and warm, and as a shelter in the winter.

snake skin

weaver bird nest

rabbit skull

GLOSSARY

absorb to soak up liquid

bark tough tree trunk skin

bask to lie in the sun

breathe take in oxygen from the air or water and give out carbon dioxide

breed to produce young

burrow a hole or tunnel dug by an animal as a home; the action of digging a burrow

cold-blooded animals whose body temperature is the same as the air or water around it

fins a flat body part that animals, such as fish, use for balance and for moving through water

gills body parts that allow animals, such as fish and tadpoles, to breathe in water

habitat the natural home of an animal or a plant

identify to find out who, what or where something is

life cycle the order of stages (from first to last) in the lifetime of an animal or plant

lungs parts of a body that allow animals, such as reptiles, birds, mammals and adult amphibians to breathe in air

mate one of a pair of breeding animals. The pair is made up of a male and a female of the same species

poisonous animals that contain a substance that can cause illness or death

pouch a pocket-like space made of skin and fur that certain types of mammal use to carry their young

predator an animal that hunts and eats other animals

prey animals that are hunted and eaten by other animals

rainforest a forest (usually in a tropical area) that gets a lot of rainfall

scale a flat object made from hard material that covers an animal's body

skeleton the bones in a body, which help support the body and move the muscles

steer point or guide something in a particular direction

tentacle bendy part of a body that is used (in this instance) for feeling the animals' surroundings

venomous an animal that is able to inject the poisonous fluid, venom

warm-blooded animals whose body temperature stays at a constant temperature

wart a small, hard, growth on top of the skin, which is usually caused by a virus

INDEX

CURIOUS FACTS

CURIOUS BEGINNINGS

People have collected objects for thousands of years. The remains of vertebrates — mainly skeletons and taxidermy skins — formed the bulk of cabinets of curiosities. These collections were made in the 1600s and 1700s by wealthy people. In time they formed the basis of the first museums.

WHAT IS A CURIOSITY BOX?

A curiosity box is a small copy of these cabinets. It is a more scientific way of displaying items than a nature table. You can group items together in their vertebrate groups of fish, amphibians, reptiles, birds and mammals. Children readily collect feathers and sometimes find bones and skulls. With care (see below) these can form the foundation of a curiosity box about animals.

YOUR CURIOSITY BOX

It's easy to make your own curiosity box. A shoebox or other small cardboard box will do! Ask an adult to help you cut long strips of card with slits cut into them. Slot them together to make lots of small sections inside your box. Place the objects you find (or photographs of them) inside the sections.

⚠️ If any specimens, such as feathers, old bones (including skulls), teeth and owl pellets are discovered, they **must** be sealed in plastic bags. **Dead animals must not be collected.** An animal curiosity box can be made entirely of photographs if you wish.

USEFUL INFORMATION AND WEBLINKS

The dissection of owl pellets is a great way to make discoveries about the bones and teeth of small vertebrates. They make excellent additions to a curiosity box. For sterilised owl pellets, and instructions for dissection and bone identification, visit: **www.owl-help.org.uk/pellet-detectives/**

For general information on practical science involving plants and animals, contact the Association for Science Education at **www.ase.org.uk** for their book, *Be Safe!* (Fourth Edition). In this book it states that items collected from the countryside, such as bones, feathers, and birds nests **that are known to be no longer in use**, may be sealed in plastic bags and containers.

ANIMALS NOTES

Here is some more information, for parents and teachers, on the animals found in this book.

What are animals?

The animals in this book are all vertebrates, which means they all have a spine. Vertebrates tend to hide away, but the easiest to spot are birds and squirrels. However, other vertebrates do leave evidence of their presence, as shown on page 5. Animals from around the world are included in this book to show the diversity of vertebrates.

Fish

Children who go fishing or who are not squeamish may like to observe the fins in a variety of fish. Fish have a basic fin pattern that comprises: the front pair of fins (pectorals), the back pair of fins (pelvic), the back or dorsal fin, the anal fin (between the anus and the tail) and the tail fin. The size, shape and position of fins may vary from species to species.

Scales are a characteristic of fish but not all fish have them. One common example of a fish without scales is the stickleback.

The salmon described here is the Atlantic salmon. When salmon return to the rivers where they were born to spawn, they may have to swim up waterfalls and avoid being eaten by bears and other predators before they can spawn. Many then die after spawning.

Amphibians

Frogs prefer damp surroundings while toads may prefer drier habitats, but both return to water to breed. Tree frogs are tiny. They live on rainforest trees and breed in small pools of water that collect in the plants that grow on tree branches.

A frog's tongue is attached to the front of its mouth, not the back as in humans. This means it can extend its tongue and use it to catch passing insects. When a frog swallows, its eyes may seem to sink into its head. This is because the back of the eyeballs form part of the roof of the frog's mouth and help push the food down its throat.

Most amphibians spend the first part of their life in water and the latter part on land. Over time the aquatic stage changes from a fish-shaped body to one with limbs. This type of change is called a metamorphosis.

Newts (a type of salamander) may be encountered on pond dipping exercises, but they also live on land outside the breeding season. On land they tend to be less colourful and blend into their surroundings. **Take care with children near water.**

The fire salamander is much larger than a newt. It has glands behind its eyes that release a poison if it is attacked by a predator. Its body colours also give a warning that it is **poisonous.**

Young caecilians are unusual amphibians because they develop inside the mother. After they are born they snuggle up to her. The mother is covered with a fatty skin, which the young pull off and eat as they grow!

Reptiles

Reptiles' scaly skin makes their bodies watertight. They lay eggs, which are really miniature 'ponds', in which the young develop. This means they do not have to breed in water like amphibians.

If a predator grabs a lizard's tail, the tail comes off and wiggles to fool the predator and help the lizard make its escape.

Snakes moult their skin in one piece, whereas lizards shed a bit at a time. A snake can locate prey more accurately with a forked tongue, as it provides two sensors instead of one. By comparing the amount of taste substances received by the two forks, the snake can work out which is receiving more and then move towards the prey. Snakes called constrictors, such as pythons, coil around their prey to stop it breathing. They don't crush it, as the damaged bones would be difficult to swallow.

Birds

Today it is believed that birds are related to reptiles – dinosaurs. Birds have scales on their legs and recent fossil finds show that some dinosaurs had feathers. Bird feathers are an easy curiosity box item to find and page 18 can be used to identify where a feather grows on a bird's body.

Birds use materials around them to make nests. You can see this yourself by putting out materials, such as dog hair or cotton thread, during the nesting season. Abandoned nests can also be observed to see if any of the materials put out have been used. Birds can be easily encouraged to feeding stations where, with luck, you may be able to observe and photograph them and listen to their songs.

Mammals

Most mammals are placental mammals, where the young develop in a womb and each one is connected to the womb wall by a placenta, which transports food and oxygen to the young. After birth the young receive milk from their mothers. In a tiny group of mammals, called monotremes, the mothers lay eggs and provide milk for their young. The platypus and the spiny anteater are both monotremes.

Pouched mammals are called marsupials and they form a group that has species in Australia and the Americas. The young spend a short time in a womb then climb out and attach themselves to a teat in a pouch to receive the rest of their nourishment.

A wide range of mammals, from rabbits and badgers to armadillos and chipmunks make burrows. Burrows give protection from predators and the weather. Voles make tunnels in the grass in meadows along which they can run, safely hidden from predators. Mammals make nests in burrows in which their newborn young can be raised. Nest materials provide insulation. The harvest mouse and squirrel are unusual; both make a nest structure outside a burrow.

Two commonly found mammal skulls in the countryside are rabbit and sheep skulls. Apart from their difference in size, they can be identified by their teeth patterns. Carnivore skulls, such as a fox, have pointed canine teeth.

In most species of deer the male grows antlers each year. They are covered in a skin called velvet, which supplies blood-carrying nutrients that are used to build the antler. When the antlers are fully grown the velvet is shed. Antlers are used in the mating season, or rut, for display and for fighting. They fall off afterwards. Horns grow steadily as the mammal matures and are not shed at the end of mating seasons.

The bones in the hand of a bat have been adapted to provide a wide area of attachment for the webbing of the wing. You may see bats flying at dusk from late spring until late autumn.